From a Cry of Anguish to a Shout of Praise

Poetry and Prose for the Hard Times in Life

Crystal J. Ortmann

WestBow
PRESS
A DIVISION OF THOMAS NELSON

Also by CRYSTAL J. ORTMANN

VROOM! VROOM!
WHAT'S THAT ANIMAL?
FASCINATING WATER

ISBN: 978-1-4497-7642-8 (sc)

Library of Congress Control Number: 2012921664

WestBow Press books may be ordered through booksellers or by contacting:

WestBow Press
A Division of Thomas Nelson
1663 Liberty Drive
Bloomington, IN 47403
www.westbowpress.com
1-(866) 928-1240

Photo credits:
Rheinfall, Switzerland by photographer, Frank B. Ortmann
Clouds and light by photographer, Frank B. Ortmann
Two friends by photographer, Barbara Lighthizer
Author photo on back cover by photographer, Frank B. Ortmann
All other photos by photographer, Crystal J. Ortmann

Printed in the United States of America

WestBow Press rev. date: 11/20/2012

To hurting people everywhere and to my husband Frank,
who portrayed the love of God as we walked together through the trials.

"'For I know the plans that I have for you,' declares the Lord, 'plans
for welfare and not for calamity to give you a future and a hope.'"
Jeremiah 29:11 (New American Standard Bible)

Table of Contents

Preface

Many years ago, as a new Christian, I felt God wanted me to write a book about pain. Recoiling at the thought, I argued . . . "But Lord, (can't you hear the whine?) I don't want any more pain. How can I write about pain if I don't experience it? Isn't there someone else?"

Now, decades later, I have fulfilled the command of my Lord. My life has had a lot of pain, both physical and emotional, but as I turned to God with everything and hung on tightly to Him through it all, He brought me from anguish to praise.

My mission is to bring the message of encouragement and hope. This hope is available to each person, no matter the circumstances or the past. Hope comes from the fact that God alone is the Source of hope and the Redeemer of each painful thing I bring to Him. He is willing and able to do the same for each life. It doesn't matter what you have done. He is waiting with open arms.

My desire is to pass this hope along to others, bringing encouragement to the body of Christ, as well as to those who do not yet know Him as their Savior.

In Christ's love,
Crystal J. Ortmann

Introduction

FROM A CRY OF ANGUISH TO A SHOUT OF PRAISE is divided into two sections. The first five chapters deal with the anguish a person may face. Chapters 6-10 deal with the praise that comes as the problems are given over to God. It is important to be honest with Him about how we feel.

If you find it difficult to share your feelings or even identify them, this poetry and prose may help you. I know reading the Psalms, where David pours out his feelings from the depth of his heart, helped me to start opening up my tattered heart to my Lord Jesus Christ. When you can do that, He can begin work in those very painful areas.

The book progresses from pain to joy. That's not to say there will never be pain again. It is a part of life. However, I know I can trust the God Who brought me through these other things to help me with my entire life. What a wonderful security.

May you be blessed and find healing in His loving arms.

Tribute to God's Grace

Broken and bent with care
Dried in spirit and soul,
I entered the doors
Of a caring, healing world.

A church,
Made up of those who love You, Lord,
Reaching out
To touch a hurting heart.

You healed through
These loving vessels.
You are filling me
With a joy I have never known.

Pouring oil on wounds so deep
I never knew were there.
You have used these vessels to bring life
Where there was only a feebly burning flame.

Thank You, Lord, for Your people.
Thank You, Lord, for Your grace.
Thank You for touching my life,
Redeeming it through people who care.

Written in gratitude to the faithful believers who have let God use them to help me find my way again.

Chapter 1:

PAIN

Sea of Agony
Pierced
Truth
An Aching Heart
A Sob
Heavenly Surgeon
Gardener of My Soul
A Teardrop
Gifts From Heaven

PACIFIC COAST IN STORM

Sea of Agony

As a dried leaf
Upon a restless wave,
I feel tossed about
Upon a sea of agony.

Pain and guilt,
Fear and terror . . .
Companions all my life.

Quiet whispers
To my heart
Speak new words of hope.

"I have come
To give new life...
Freedom from the sea of agony."

"It won't be easy,
But I'll be there
All along the way."

Tiny seeds of trust
He plants.
Faith where there was doubt.

He won't leave me there
To toss upon
The sea of agony.

He has plans
For my life...
He loves me, that's for sure.

I gladly give my
Yes to Him,
And leave behind things that destroy.

Pierced

Pierced......
Great drops of hurt
Flowing as blood
From the wound in my heart.

Painful, hurting words from a so-called friend,
Targeting a very tender area
Of my soul.

I ran to my Lord,
My hurt to Him outpoured.
He touched my heart,
His healing to impart.

Resting upon His ready breast,
I find repose,
I find His rest.

Trusting only in Him
To make me whole
And give relief.

He will take each hurtful thing
That causes pain
And make it gain.

Truth

White hot pain . . .
Hurt . . . going deep
But, cleansing as it goes,
Isolating a tumor of sin . . .
Then, setting it free
To be healed.

Pain came in words from a friend;
Truly a friend
Who told me what I was doing
Hurt others.

Pain . . .because it hurt to hear the truth.
Pain . . . coupled with angry feelings . . .
Wishing to inflict some pain in return,
Yet, held in check...to be spoken of with God.

Then - the deepest pain of all
As I faced myself,
Because I know it's true.

God makes new life to grow
From severed parts.
New and better life,
Using this person and that
To shape and smooth me
Into His image.

An Aching Heart

Wrapping loving arms of comfort
Around this aching soul,
My God and my Redeemer
Speaks to my breaking heart.

He loves me with unfathomable love.
I sense it through the tears.
The lonely parts inside me
He sees and knows and hears.

He loves me with a love so pure,
So full of grace and truth...
He loves me, yes, He loves me!
My inner wounds are soothed.

Oh God, I worship You,
In my imperfect way.
I love You with my impure love.
I long to go Your way.

I thank You for those loving arms,
The ones that say, "I care."
With freely flowing tears,
I reach to You in prayer.

You lift me when I'm feeling low,
You touch me when I'm glad.
You know the depths to which I go
When I am feeling sad.

My Lord, I worship You this day
In poem, in song, in prayer.
Please help my life to show Your love,
To show how much You care.

I do not need to buy Your love
By good things that I do.
I only need to cling to You

A Sob

A sob tears loose
From a heart filled with pain . . .
Wracking my body
Again and again.

Always outside, it seems,
Looking in...
A barrier stands
Between others and me.

Jesus says "Come,
Come right here to My side.
Bring Me your sorrow.
In Me you can hide."

"I will break down
The walls in your life.
I see your longing
To be free from strife."

"Loneliness, sorrow,
Chaos and hurt,
Leave you breathless,
Feeling like dirt."

"I come to heal,
To give and restore.
Come to My side, child,
You'll want no more."

"It will come slowly . . .
A few steps each day.
I promise to meet your needs
In My unique way."

"Look into My loving face,
Find your worth in Me.
Circumstances in your life cannot bring you peace."

"Only I can heal you,
Love you through and through.
Only I can truly love
No matter what you do."

"Trust in My mercy,
Trust in My power.
Let Me be your Guide
Through each and every hour."

"I am helping you to find
The place where you should be.
Do not be discouraged, child,
Place your trust in Me."

Heavenly Surgeon

White hot pains
Course through my soul
As my heavenly Surgeon
Makes me whole.

With perfect poise
He severs within
Things that would bind me,
Troubles and sin.

Draining the boils
Of bitterness and pain,
Healing the scars
That dormant have lain.

They were causing me grief,
Deep in my soul,
He saw me and pitied.
Desired to make whole.

Requiring from me
Merely my "Yes,"
He gently removes
What causes distress.

My heavenly Surgeon,
With touch that is true,
Desires to heal,
To give life anew.

He longs to take
Each crippled part,
Healing and straightening,
Giving new heart.

There is no illness,
No pain so severe
My heavenly Father cannot repair.

Gardener of My Soul

Weeding out those places of my heart
That cause me pain
And rob my joy.

Weeding all the ugly thoughts and deeds,
With certain hand,
My Lord does work.

Pain, oft severe,
As He severs here and there,
Healing comes
With a peace that calms my heart.

Trusting in the Gardener of my soul,
I let Him in
To weed my life.

Taking all the interwoven roots,
With practiced hand,
He sets me free.

Stubborn and tangled . . .
Fighting all the way,
Roots of sin He exposes
To the light of day.

Oh my Lord,
I trust in You . . .
The Gardener of my soul.

A Teardrop

A teardrop glistening in the light
Slides gently down her cheek
Dropping silently into her lap.

Hot, burning tears . . .
Starting with brimming eyes,
Spilling over slowly at first,
Then cascading in ever increasing torrents
As her grief breaks through.

In spite of the pain,
In spite of the hurt,
There is beauty in the tears.
Reflecting the light, they sparkle
As much as any diamond.

Tears,
God's cleansing jewels . . .
Bringing relief to her hurting heart.

Gifts from Heaven

Sunbeams boldly touch
Diamond-laden trees,
Flashing light of myriad hues.

Sparkling droplets,
Glorious, refreshing,
Life-giving, quenching
Thirst of plant and soil.

God, You let rain fall on our lives . . .
Washing, giving life, quenching thirst,
Causing us to sparkle as
Your love shines through the sorrow.

Tears and raindrops . . .
Heavenly gifts of
Untold beauty and life.

Chapter 2:

FEAR

Released

Her soul was in fear-shrouded darkness,
Terror a familiar friend.
The Savior came into that darkness
To pain, He's putting an end.

A small child
So frightened and tortured,
With no possible means of escape,
Fights against walls of a prison,
A prison she did not make.

Jesus, the wonderful Savior,
Tells her "Give it to Me."
Longing to make this child whole,
He wants to heal and set free.

Reluctantly, she opened the door,
At first, only a crack.
So often ones she had trusted
Had stabbed her in the back.

The Jesus she encountered
Was not like any of them.
He was faithful, loving and honest
He always meant what He said.

Oh, but trusting was so very hard.
Each step a painful thing.
Yet, each step brought healing and comfort,
Trust, growth, and freedom to sing.

The past still controls much of the present,
But joy is now part of her life.
He's releasing her from her bondage
Bringing peace to the raging strife.

Whispers from the Past

At unexpected times
When my guard is down,
Whispers from the past
Steal into my thoughts unbidden.

Rage, fear, terror, shame,
Passions deep
Without a name
Leave me spent and weak.

But, God is near.
He is healing,
All is in His hands.

In the Dark Hour

In the dark hour
Before dawn,
Comes the mass of fears
Unchecked.

It is hard
To think or pray.
All seems muddled,
All seems gray.

I come to You, Lord,
All my fears I outpour...
Then comes Your light
Into my gloom.

Calmer of the Seas

Seas threaten
To break over me.
Fear clutches my soul.

Turmoil and fear
Lurk everywhere
Trying to gain a hold.

My tiny boat
Tossed all about
By things beyond my control.

With eyes on the waves,
Close to going under,
A whisper speaks to me . . .

"Turn your eyes to Me,
Not what you can see.
I am the Calmer of the seas."

Eyes on my Savior,
Water seems less rough,
As He makes me whole.

Jesus, my Jesus!
Calmer of the seas,
And Calmer of my soul.

Terror Stalks

Terror stalks. It is dark, quiet . . . nothing to be heard but rhythmic breathing. With tiny darts, it edges its way into my half-asleep mind. I awaken and then it comes with sudden forcefulness, nearly strangling my breath.

Clear thoughts are impossible when this enemy attacks.
I then know the reality of sheer panic and writhe beneath its suffocating hand.

Tiny droplets of sweat bead on my brow. Sleep flees. My thoughts are chaotic. I cry out silently to the Lord. I cling to Him as a drowning sailor clings to a broken mast. His words of comfort and protection speak to me from deep within and quiet me. He has told me He will never go from me. He is there day and night to guard me from all evil. No one and nothing can cause His love to fail.

With His peace blanketing me, the warmth of sleep overtakes my weary frame and I sleep, unafraid.

He is with me. I am safe in His hands.

From Fear to Hope

Deep in my being
Fear rages.
Clawing, maiming, tearing . . .
Waiting for a moment when I am weak
To rear its ugly head.

Fear is a many-headed dragon.
It doesn't let up,
Until the conquerer faith moves in.
Then the angry beast is stilled . . .
Rendered harmless.

Peace takes over then
With a calm assurance.
A quietness, a gentle whisper saying
"All is well. You are in my hands.
I will not let you go,
For I purchased you with My blood."

Faith falters again, bringing torment,
Then reasserts itself, bringing peace.
Then comes torment again.
Where is faith?
Quietly, it steals over me
As I lift my eyes once more to Jesus.

Deep within He whispers words of love.
He reassures me there is no circumstance
Bigger than His ability to handle it.
Nothing can cause Him to withdraw His love.
Peace comes then . . . quiet, comforting,
Wrapping my inner self with rest.

Confusion is gone.
Clarity returns.
Hope is there.
I am in His hands.
He will bring me through.

Chapter 3:

LONELINESS

Lonely
Where Are You, Friend?

MALHEUR NATIONAL WILDLIFE REFUGE OREGON

Lonely

Sitting in my chair
Loneliness consumes me
As I wait for the phone to ring.

Longing fills my heart
For a friend . . .
Someone with whom to laugh and be myself.

The terror is deep
That a friend I cannot keep.
Maybe something's wrong with me.

Longing cries out and
Makes me want to shout:
I am longing for a friend!

I'm frightened to reach out
For fear of disappointing
Or, being disappointed.

"Please Lord," I cry,
"Help me to try.
Help me trust You to provide."

In those lonely times
Faced with all of my fears,
I'm forced to turn with them to God.

As He sets free,
Hope is given me
And I find the way to health and joy.

He'll bring those friends.
My heart He will mend.
Speaking to me new words of life.

I need to listen,
Let Him work,
Let Him guide me to a friend.

His word is true.
He will bring that friend.
He will help me learn to be one too.

God, my perfect Friend,
Speaks His love to me,
Reassuring and lifting my heart.

Father, Friend and Guide
Ever at my side...
He will provide for me.....

A friend.

Where Are You, Friend?

Pain goes deep
As I reflect
How little time
People have for me.

"I'm so busy!"
"My schedule's too tight!"
Is the explanation
I too often hear.

I long to hear my telephone ring...
For someone to ask me how I am.
For an invitation
For coffee or tea.

It isn't important
What we do...
Rather knowing that someone cares
To be with me.

It seems as if
I am the one
Who phones...invites...
Or remains alone

Dear God, I want to be a friend.
To reach out to others...
To care for them...

But...isn't it right
That they could see,
I'd like to know
They're seeking me?

Self-pity is there...
It's the way that I feel...
Even so,
The hurt is real.

Friendship,
A very precious thing . . .
Give and take
On both sides too.

Not being
Too busy
To care about you.

I'm tired of calling,
Inviting,
Making the first move.

So, dear Lord,
This prayer I send.
A question, really,

"Where are you, friend?"

Chapter 4:

STRUGGLES WITH SIN

Nothing Without Love

Warmth . . . pure, clean warmth,
Wrapping its tendrils softly around my being,
Reaching to depths unplumbed
As He is allowed to rule.

Undeserved love...
Love from the Father,
Through the suffering of His Son...
Love for me and for you.

Cold comes too . . .
Bitter cold within, when I withdraw my being
From His Lordship.
Desolate wasteland . . .
Barren and cold.

As His love warms the bitter cold away,
I, too, am able to love.
He loves me in my ugliness.
Can I do any less for others?

Yet, I do. I judge and condemn.
I withdraw with hurt feelings.
Without His love,
Life is not worthwhile.

Without His love flowing through me
I am nothing.
All my great plans of doing something for God
Fall in empty heaps.

Lord, help me to love.
Help me to look beyond my petty hurts,
Beyond dirty faces
And dirty lives and love
With Your love.

Logs

With critical spirit
I reviewed the faults
Of those around me.

"Oh, Lord," I prayed,
"Please help them be
Just like me."

He softly spoke
To my heart
Tender words like these . . .

"Let Me take the logs
From your eyes
Then you will truly see."

Shame covered me
As my thoughts were revealed:
Critical, judging, jealous, and prideful.

It isn't wrong to do what I feel is right...
It isn't wrong to pray
For those whose lives seem wrong.

It is only wrong to judge by looking with contempt.
Prayer and a clean heart
Are the tools I must use to right a wrong.

I must live the things I see as right.
Cleanse me, Lord and make sincere my desire
To pray for those in need.

Take the forest from my sight.
Let me pray in purity of heart.
Keep me true to things I've learned.

Teach me how to pray
For Your pure wisdom with no logs to bar the view.

WESTERN OREGON WAYSIDE

Stones

While crossing a rippling brook
I stooped down to take a look.
I found there many different stones
Of varied color tones.

Then spoke my precious Lord to me,
"Through these stones, I'm teaching thee.
Some are flat and some are round,
Some lie there and make no sound.

Some are rough and some are smooth,
Some are steadfast and do not move.
Don't you see, these stones, dear heart
Have a lesson to impart?

In My body, there are stones
With different tints and varied tones.
With diverse shapes and unlike sizes,
With needs oft no one recognizes.

With different levels in their walk,
Some are rough ones and some balk;
Some who merely stay in place,
Some who need a faster pace.

Some who cut and some who hurt,
Some still clinging to the dirt.
All need guidance and My love
To fit the plan that's from above.

If some of My stones cause you pain
Others will come to soothe again.
A beautiful mosaic My stones can be
If they're bonded together in Me."

Disorder

All around me I see disorder and confusion.
Dishes waiting to be washed . . .
Clothes strewn about . . .
Clutter everywhere.
This is good, for disorder reminds me of what I have:
A family,
Enough food,
Warm clothes and blankets,
A roof above my head,
Love.
It takes only a short amount of time to clear it away,
To put it right and back where it belongs.
A feeling of accomplishment arises out of the day-by-day tasks,
A deep-down fulfillment and a warm, satisfied feeling of caring for my
family.
In my mind, and life there is also clutter, disorder and confusion.
God, my great, loving Father and Housekeeper of my soul is clearing
that away too.
He is taking away the rubbish and washing, dusting, sweeping out all
the unimportant, mending the broken and torn and putting all in proper
order.
There is much disorder and much confusion and, so the process goes
slowly, that I might experience new life, little by little.
A life of love, peace, sunshine, trust in dark times, concern for my fellow
man, daily loving, forgiving and being forgiven.
Daily growing closer to my family and my Lord,
For this, I thank You.

Destructive Companion

Worry
My companion from earliest years
Destructive, deadly
Yet, so dear to me.

"I don't want to give it up!
It's my friend!
A part of me!"

The Savior gently whispers,
"It only does you harm."

Frightened at losing
An integral part of my life,
I pull the walls around me.
Perhaps He will not see.

The Savior once more whispers,
"I want to set you free."

"But, Lord!" I argue,
"It's only worry...so small a thing.
My friend, my companion from early days."

The Savior speaks so gently,
"Think of just how harmless this 'friend' is.
Headaches, joylessness, robbing you of your peace,
Your happiness, consuming your thoughts, giving ulcers . . .
Is it really your friend?"

So hard to admit,
A crutch,
A cancer of my soul . . .
That's what worry really is.

Not a friend but a destructive force.
Take it, Lord. I'm ready for You to make me whole.

A Clean Heart

Brimming with success,
My heart filled with pride,
The Savior called me
To His side.

"I love you too much
To allow you to stray.
I want you to serve Me,
Not go your own way."

"But, Lord!" I exclaimed,
"It feels so fine . . .
All the attention
That now is mine."

Deep in my heart,
I knew He was right,
But, the longing for praise
Put up such a fight.

I knelt at His feet
Chastened and sore.
Forgiveness I asked for
And so much more.

Before His throne
I saw wrong that I do....
Proud, vain and boastful,
Critical too.

His Word says we can
Be tested by praise.
I failed this one, Lord, but,
Thanks for Your grace.

I'm thankful You love me so much
You will show
When I start to wander and bring me back home.

"Cleanse me, dear Father. Please help me to live
For Your glory only,
My sins please forgive."

As He does the cleansing,
Giving me a new start,
True contentment and joy
Flood my now clean heart.

I ask for the wisdom,
To see when I err.
The Father is faithful.
For me He will care.

Caring means more than
Protection and love.
It also means chastening
From the Father above.

Unholy desires,
Deeds of the flesh,
He will help conquer
At my request.

"Lord, keep me open
Help me hear Your call
To bring You glory...
To be my all."

Frantic

Soft fingers of quiet
Steal into the secret places
Of my heart. "Oh God," I cry.
"It's too much for me.
The longing of my heart
Is to have time for others...
A listening ear.
A moment to share and show I care."

I hate the frantic pace of life.
It seems an enemy to me,
Attacking all that is good
And healthy. Friends don't have time....
Loneliness invades.
Activity of every sort
Replaces quiet times, alone.

When one has time it seems somehow wrong.
"Lazy...goof-off, wasting time! There are
So many needs crying to be met!"
Lord, I can't help wondering...
How many less needs would there be
If more people had time for a quiet moment
With family and friends and You?

I despise the frantic pace
Which causes each to see one's schedule as a god.
No time to chat or smell a flower.
No understanding when one must wait.
"Me first!" the theme of such a way of life.

I may be only one, Lord, but
I cannot justify rushing to and fro
When it means I have no time for
The things that really count. . . .

People and
You.

Hectic

Feelin' kind of crowded in my head.
I look for space
To think and pray.

Things just sort of whirlin' round my mind.
I need some time
To think and pray.

Life has so much stress,
Pressure everywhere,
But, I can turn to Jesus
With every hurt and care.

Feelin' good because today I know,
He'll lift those clouds,
He'll make me whole.

Not So Fast!

Noise, confusion, and clutter rage in my mind.
Feeling caught in a whirlwind
Unable to unwind.
Unable to sleep or to relax,
Unable to think.....
I must go quietly...
Carefully listening.
So many immovable mountains all around me.
How can I give, when I am just trying to hang on?

Sensitive, hurt, angry,
Caught like a cornered animal
Seeking escape.

The only true escape from one's problems is to
face them, turning in faith to God,
pouring out the heart to Him, and
letting Him sort out the mess.

God...the God of peace and order...not of confusion.
Big enough to control the universe,
Bigger than war and hate, yet,
Big enough to care about the smallest detail of my life...
the pain...the hurt...the resentment.
Big enough to understand
And want to cleanse what makes me unhappy from within.

I'm tired...feeling pressed on every side....
Still the gentle whisper comes,
"Not so fast, child.
Wait on Me.
Let Me give you peace."

Coming with the Questions of My Heart

Coming with the questions of my heart,
With head bowed low,
All my cares and worries to impart,
I come to You, I come to You.

Your arms are always open,
Your ears always hear.
You're never too busy
To show that You care.

Lord, You fill that empty place inside,
A void that was always there.
Bringing me the sense of hope and love,
All things You gladly with me share.

I love You, Lord.
I never knew
That life could be so sweet
Lived with You.

Thank You for caring.
Thank You for sharing.
Thank You for dying for me.

Distractions

So many distractions
To draw me away
From serving the Lord
In my unique way.

Fears, doubts and busyness
Pluck at my thoughts,
Leaving me empty,
My mind distraught.

Lord, keep me focused
On Your will for my life.
Trying to please others
Just increases my strife.

Give me the courage
To walk in Your light,
My eyes on You, Savior,
The will to do right.

So often I stumble
As my heart goes astray.
Let You be my Center,
For this I pray.

Sins from the past
Or fears for the future
Rob me of victory, and
Keep me unsure.

You, Lord, give power
To overcome sin.
Fear and guilt vanish
When You dwell within.

Please, Lord, I pray now
Take control of each thought.
Help me to live life
Each day as I ought.

Fulfilling Your plan,
Overcoming the past,
Trusting the future,
For Your love will last.

Distractions come daily,
But they needn't succeed
In robbing my victory,
For in You, I'm free.

With honest confession,
I bring them to You.
Drawing on Your strength
To carry me through

Lord, purify me.
Make Your thoughts my own.
Bring to maturity
Those seeds You have sown.

This is my prayer, Lord,
To bring glory to You.
Take all that I offer,
Help me to stay true.

It takes time to learn this.
So often I fall.
But, You, Lord are faithful
In spite of it all.

Chapter 5:

HEALING

Healing in My Soul

Light streaks through my darkness
Chains break apart.
Iron shackles shatter
As Christ heals my heart.

I turned to Him in terror,
Saying, "Lord, please set me free!
Help me face my fears, God,
And conquer my enemy."

God is, oh, so faithful.
My fears He hears and sees.
Each tiny prayer He answers,
From bondage He relieves.

The pain, severe, yet healing,
Causes courage, in spite of fear.
The love my Savior gives me
Redeems each sorrowful tear.

So many years I've tried, Lord,
To make my own self clean,
To cover over stains and soil
To hide the things unseen.

I know now, Lord, I cannot
Make my own life whole.
Only trusting in Your mercy
Can there be healing in my soul.

Based on Psalm 107

A Tender Heart

A tender heart, O Lord,
Is what I asked of You.
Despite the hurt of life,
Let hard and bitter feelings not erode
The tender softness of Your love in me.

God, I brought my life to You.
I stood before You and laid it all out.
Ripped and torn,
Eyes red from weeping, and`
Asked for a childlike heart.

No matter what happens in my life,
Please keep me soft inside
That is my plea...
And He's doing it for me.

Inspired by 2 Chronicles 34:27

Relief

Relief fills my soul,
I feel now I'm whole.
My heart wants
To sing and shout!

My God,
He reached down,
Changed my rags
To His gown.

He lifted me
From the pit.
My life He made whole,
He healed my soul.

I love Him
With all of my heart.

Although so much was wrong
My heart now has a song
Of forgiveness,
Of healing, and new life.

It's for you, too, friend.
He loves to the end.
There's nothing for you
He won't do.

He'll give you new life,
Put an end to that strife
Which has robbed you
And kept you so down.

He not only loves,
He heals and forgives.
He gives grace
The new life to live.

I thought it was the end,
Didn't know He was my Friend,
Didn't know how much
He cared for me.

He'll be a Friend for you,
Giving you life anew,
Putting song and joy
Into your heart.

No matter what you've done
Who you've been, where you've gone,
He redeems, pardons, and
Forgives.

He lifts you from the pit,
The misery in which you sit.
Healing, restoring,
Giving new life within.

Trust Him now, I pray...
Don't waste another day.
Let Him begin
Your life to heal.

Tell Him of your fear,
Show Him your tears,
Your doubt and lack of trust.
Tell Him how you feel, that truly is a must.

He's the only Friend I know
Who can understand you so:
The pain, the bitter feelings,
The times when you fall.

You can trust His love for you
To bring you safely through.
This I can guarantee,
Because He's doing it for me.

From Darkness to Light

Dark, murky clouds
Hang over my head.
My vision is cloudy.
It's so hard to see!

Despair fills my heart.
I long for a light
To show me the way,
Because it's so hard to see!

Wrapped in the darkness,
I feel the touch of a hand,
A hand so gentle and sweet.
Still, it's so hard to see!

"You don't have to see
When I'm leading the way,"
He spoke to my troubled heart,
"You need only hang onto My hand."

Through the darkness I walked,
Hand in hand with my Lord.
With the light of His Word,
I began to see.

I came out of the darkness,
Led by His light,
Out to the sun and fresh breeze.
I cried out, "Now I can see!"

He walks with me in darkness and light.
His Word illumines my way.
Daylight or night, hand in hand with my Lord,
I cry out now "I can see!"

Based on Job 29:3b (NASB)

The Shepherd's Near

The Shepherd's near.
I know He's there,
When I am plagued
With fear and care.

When doubts assail,
When I fret,
When painful tears
Alone I've wept...

The Shepherd's near.

When old and new hurts fester there,
He reminds I'm in His care.
He binds each wound, pours oil upon
The very thing in me that's wrong.

The Shepherd's near...
I will rejoice,
And shout my praises
With my voice!

The Shepherd's near.

Chapter 6:

HIS CALLING

You Called Me, Lord
Our Calling
Called to Care

You Called Me, Lord

Based on Psalm 138:3, 7a

I called to Him
In my distress,
A cry, a muffled sob.

The pain so great
There were no words...
Just reaching toward my God.

He answered me,
He heard my cry,
He brought me strength within.

My soul He touched
With strength that day,
He loosed the cords of sin.

This life on earth
Has many trials,
Troubles, hurts and pain.

Though I must sometimes
Walk through them,
I'll never be the same.

My Lord is there
To walk with me,
Reviving, giving peace.

He'll bring me through
With loving care.
From fear I'll be released.

You called me, Lord,
To be Your child
Your gifts You freely give.

Your one desire
Is that I trust
As through my life You live.

Our Calling

As clouds absorb and radiate the light of the sun, they bring color, warmth and joy to the heart. As Christians, our calling is like that of the clouds.... to absorb and radiate the Light of Jesus.....bringing color, warmth and joy to the hearts of those around us.

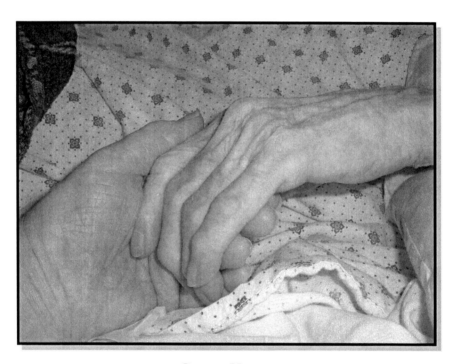

CARING HANDS

Called to Care

Ragged lives cry out
"Someone care for us!"
Chasing phantoms which promise peace,
But only break the heart.

Caged within sin's prison,
Aching souls attempt
Without success to
Free themselves.

On knees bent in prayer,
I plead with God above,
To save the ones I love,
And free them for all time.

God sits in seeming silence,
Until the time is ripe.
His Spirit tugs those heartstrings
Until they cry for Him.

Called to care...
To extend God's love
To those caught in
Impenetrable walls of sin.

Through caring prayer
And the touch of love,
God is able to break down
Merciless barriers.

Called to care....
To extend love
To ragged, dirty lives
Knowing, but for Him, there go I.

Chapter 7:

PRAYER

The Filled Cup

An empty cup I brought to Him,
Stretched high to catch it all.

Amused, He gently murmured,
"It is already full.."

"Daily I am filling,
Daily you receive."

"Only look inside your cup.
See what I have given."

With doubtful heart, I mumbled,
"I know it isn't full."

Looking in, my eyes were opened,
Seeing gifts so freely given.

There was healing for my hurt,
Love for who I am,

Acceptance, joy and mercy...
Peace, release and calm.

It was full to overflowing!
My Savior wasn't wrong.

Accepting His full cup with thanks,
I humbly knelt to pray,

"Thank You, Lord for filling me,
Each and every day."

His filling for my cup is there,
Whenever I will pray.

In the Seclusion of Dawn

The quiet seclusion of dawn wraps around me like a cloak.
I find silence, peace, time to communicate with my God.
There is rebirth, hope rekindled, quiet soothing of the frightened,
painful places within.
"Oh God," my spirit cries, "You are so close. At dawn, I seem to sense
Your Presence so much more!" It could be because there are not so many
distractions . . . but then, this has always been my favorite time of day.

My mind is fresh and uncluttered, for I have just rid myself of unwanted
burdens. I feed my spirit on His Word. There has been no time for new
problems to present themselves.

How I love this quiet hour. How I love my Lord and the time spent in
His Presence, this sweet gentle communion. I want to offer my whole
being to His service.

Thank You Lord for quiet hours of meditation and communion
with You.

Cozy

Pouring rain, cozy inside . . .
A little quiet, a time to pray . . .
To touch God's heart
And let Him touch mine.

My Favorite Time of Day

There is a special moment in my day that brings a thrill and a secret peace to my heart. It's a small allotment of time, but like no other time, I am free. I am close to Jesus. It is quiet. It is the moment when I meet Him face to face. He fills my drained cup and gives me strength to meet the challenges of another day.

I went to Him at one time out of fear, because I felt I should. One day, I told Him the truth - He Who is the Truth and knew my heart already. "I don't want to pray. I don't want to talk to you. I don't want to go through the motions just so I won't feel guilty all day!"

Deep in my heart, He lovingly gave me assurance that the only fellowship He seeks is what is given willingly. He desires openness and honesty from me: whether in a chat with Him as Friend, or when I am brimming with love, anxiety or need of any kind. He wants it all poured out with a sincere heart.

When that moment came, the bonds were severed to the old lip-service. I entered into a new and exciting relationship with my Lord. Now, I usually long for those moments of peace and quiet, when we settle down for our heart to heart talk. I share my deepest thoughts and He listens. He shares with me through His Word, through a sweet, gentle urging deep in my being, and I listen to Him.

Slowly new life is forming within me. Life that is crying out to live, breathe, feel, laugh, cry, love and believe more.

Can you see why this is my favorite time of day?

I Sit in the Stillness

I sit alone in the stillness of early morning. Outside my window, a strong spring wind twists the branches, contorting them in bizarre antics. Occasionally soft rain spatters lightly on the windowpane. Grey clouds, pregnant with spring rains, envelop the surrounding countryside.

At times like these, I feel a sense of comfort because God is there. From my warm apartment perched where I can see so well, the panorama of the awakening day unfolds.

My desk is a place of comfort too. Paper, pens, and books make up this world in which I feel secure, and as excited as the child who gets his first notebook and box of crayons for school.

I am ready to burst with a need to write and pour it all out. This is the sometimes downside of being creative.

Often wishing I were different, more placid, less flighty, not so sensitive and emotional. Wishing at times I didn't "feel" so much. However, the thought has then come to me, these things aren't bad in themselves. It's what I do with them that makes the difference.

So what if I am a dreamer and thinker? So what if I'm not so "down-to-earth" and practical? How much pleasure is added to the world of "common sense" because of a touch of beauty is added. How dull life would be if we were all practical, *common sense* folk. How chaotic if we were all extremely creative. How wonderful when we can mix together and accept one another as we are.

We each have so much to offer. Lord, teach us to complement each other. Use me Lord. Show me what You would have me do. Help me to cease looking around at others, and comparing, judging, feeling pride or insecurity. Help us, Your children, to accept one another, working in unity to further Your kingdom.

Early Morning

I love the sound of the silence.
Its soothing, comforting way
Speaks to me of peace and joy
To last me through the day.

I love the peaceful feeling
When silence enters in.
The early morning time with God
Brings strength and power within.

This early time of silence
Wraps round me as a shawl,
Soothing, speaking softly
Till my spirit hears His call.

The Master speaks so quietly
I need the peace to hear
The gently words of love
He whispers in my ear.

At His Feet

Precious and sweet,
As one sits at His feet,
Are the thoughts
Of the blessings He gives.

Fellowship, love
From heaven above,
Security, comfort,
And, Him.

Even in fear
When falls a tear,
He is there by your side.

Giving you hope,
He helps you to cope
With whatever comes into life.

You are never alone.
You can run to His throne,
Tell Him all of your doubts and fears.

Outstretched arms He holds
Open to you...
Run to them, don't delay.

He's waiting for you
With a welcoming heart.
Waiting, your heart to win.

Run to Him now,
And, if you allow,
He'll free you from burdens of sin.

Nothing too bad,
Too dreadful, or sad.
He's not shocked by things you have done.

Learning His way
To freedom and health
That's His desire for you.

He'll free you from your past
Give peace that will last.
He will bless your life with true wealth.

Wealth that you seek
Is not of what I speak.
He gives what really satisfies.

Treasured friends and true love,
Wisdom from above,
Contentment, no matter your condition.

The Lord of Whom I tell
Wants to make your sore heart well.
Won't you let Him in to your life?

Let Me Live for You

When, in this early hour
I gaze upon Your face,
All my worries slip away,
Gone without a trace.

Lord, how I love You.
Father, Spirit, Son.
You have conquered all on earth,
Every battle won.

Lord, I cannot tell You,
How much You mean to me.
I can only live for You
A life, by You set free.

Let me live for You, Lord.
Turn my every thought to You.
Let the love You give each day
Guide all I say and do.

Sweet Silence

There is sweetness in the silence
Of the early morning.
It wraps around me, bringing peace
To ragged edges of my soul.

Loneliness does not afflict me
At this golden hour.
Each pore and cell revives.
As I am soothed, strength flows in.

It's that lovely morning hour,
The best of all the day.
A time to think, a time to pray,
A time to get in touch with God.

Out my window
I see lightly falling snow.
Wind, so crisp and fresh
Blows vitality into all.

Creativity rises within and
Shouts to be heard!
Spontaneous words of praise
Pour forth unto the Lord.

Touched by beauty
In morning hours,
Sweet silence.
A gift to me from God.

Prayer

In quiet times I feel the pull
Of God's own loving hand...
For when I stand before His throne,
His hearing I command.

Alone, through Christ, I come to Him,
His mercy to implore.
To fix my eyes upon His face,
His being to adore.

He does not see my filthy rags,
Or, bad things I have done.
He sees me through the Living Christ,
Who is the Holy One.

He is my strength, my power, my might,
My fortress in the storm.
From Him need nothing be held back,
His love is deep and warm.

He isn't shocked by things I've thought,
Or things I've done or said.
He knows me, oh, so very well,
And, how I should be led.

Oh, precious, lovely quiet time,
With the Lord of all.
I leave this time with newfound strength
To face the daily call.

A bit of Him rubs off on me,
As at His throne I pray.
My quiet time, my time of prayer,
Most precious time of day.

This prayer of mine, not always long,
Not always filled with grace;
Oft just a whisper, at times a cry, or a tearstained face.
He hears it all and loves me still.
The wonder makes me sing...
For through the quiet times of prayer,
I come to know my King.

He Hears

What a precious thing it is
To go to God in prayer.
What a treasure in my life,
All things with Him to share!

I never need to worry that
He won't have time for me.
He hears, He sees, He listens
To every word and plea.

I love to spend the time with Him
In early morning hours.
The quiet and the peace lead
To closeness that is ours.

Oh God, the riches I possess
Surpass the richest king.
My Lord, my God, my Savior,
To me, You're everything.

I love You, Lord,
And come with brimming heart
To Your throne of mercy
My secrets to impart.

Thank You, Lord, You're always there
A haven in every storm.
You hear, You see, You listen...
You're my eternal home.

RAINY DAY

Little Things

A droplet sparkling in the rain.
The smile when love breaks through the pain.
Soft gentleness of a kiss from the one you love.
Tender words spoken when you feel down.
The honest acceptance by another.
A friend...one who listens and still loves.
The sun, after days of gloom, spilling gold in every room
Talents...always there, yet newly discovered.
The love of your child.
The earnestness of your husband as he shares his hopes and fears.
A little compliment dropped your way.
The smile of another that made the day.
The touch of a compassionate hand.
Walking through the sand barefoot.
The sound of wind in the trees....
Sometimes a breeze, sometimes causing awe.
A glass of water.
Aroma of coffee.
Doing something for others, especially when they don't know who did it.
Making someone happy.
The scent of fresh-baked bread.
Roses, violets, lilacs...all the beauty of sight and smell.
Blue sky, fluffy white clouds.
Walking where it isn't crowded.
Laughter.
Peace.
A good book.
The smell of the forest.
So many little things planned by God to bring us happiness.

Thank You, Father.

A Stillness Deep

There is a stillness deep
Coming from the steel blue of the sky...
Touching every star with diamond-fire brilliance,
Making the very light shimmer and sparkle.

It is the stillness of bitter cold.
Beautiful, yet deadly to those caught unaware.

How grateful I am for my warm home,
For hot coffee, a nourishing meal,
Warm clothing to protect me from
The deepest cold.

I am rich. I am blessed.
All I ever need to make me happy is at my disposal.
There is the hope of healing, of rectifying past mistakes.
The hope of becoming whole.

More than these, I cannot ask.
I can glory in the beauty of the cold, and pray for
Those who cannot.

A Slender Thread

A life held by a slender thread
In throes of anguish and of dread,
Denies the need of Christ.

A life so full of promise rich
Sees no need for help.
Instead, reels under the pain and confusion,
Often self-inflicted.

O sacred Lord, reach out Your hand,
And touch this troubled soul.
Extend Your hand and heal his life.
Touch and make him whole.

Let Him see his need of You,
Show him that You're real.
Touch his very inner self
And, with that touch You'll heal.

You're the home he needs to find,
The anchored haven fair.
Touch his life; please lead him home.
Let him know You care.

Chapter 8:

GROWING IN CHRIST

He'll See You Through

I came to Him all soiled and gray.
In His great love, He let me stay.
He drew me close to His scarred side
And said, "My child, for you I died."

"But, Lord!" I cried in bitterest shame,
"I've tried so hard to bear Your name.
I've tried to do it perfectly,
Attempting to be what I should be."

"But, Lord, O Lord!" I cried again,
"I've failed, yes, failed Your perfect plan.
I've been selfish, I've been mean,
I've had MY way . . . I'm not so clean."

He spoke to me with voice so meek,
"It is good My will to seek,
But, you must know that you each day
Will make mistakes along the way."

"That is when I rejoice . . .
When I hear your pleading voice
Crying to Me in utter shame
Because you failed to exalt My name."

"I am there not just to save.
I died and rose from the grave
In order to set your spirit free,
To cleanse, to pardon and to heal."

"Daily I'm there to intercede,
Daily hearing the prayers you plead.
Rejoicing when you call My name,
Every day, I cleanse your shame."

It seems so great, this love He gives.
Each day I'm thankful that He lives
To love, to heal, to pardon me,
To give me inner liberty.

I give Him my heart
His grace He'll impart
Making me healthy and free.

Lift a voice in praise, my heart.
This lesson will my Lord impart . . .
He's not there just to be praised.
For pardon He was also raised.

To put my brokenness aright,
To help me walk in His pure light,
He comforts, binds, loves and guides.
He'll always be there at my side.

He knows I've failed, for that He grieves,
Though, He stands ready to intercede.
He's my most perfect friend
Who'll be beside me to the end.

No greater friend could there be
Than Jesus who died on Calvary.
As I place my hand in His with trust
He removes the grime and dust.

He who loves without a qualm
Will provide the healing balm.
Grace and pardon He gives anew.
As I trust in Jesus, He sees me through.

No One Beyond His Love

There is no one beyond His love and care,
Nothing outside of His interest,
He's willing with all to share.

Despair clings to you,
You think you're no good.
Life seems so hopeless somehow.

Jesus is waiting
With outstretched arms
Waiting for you to come.

His is a love
Perfect and pure.
He's not offended by you.

He wants to touch you,
Heal all your wounds,
Make your life something new.

I was despairing,
Drowning in grief,
Sinking in self-pity and gloom.

Jesus came in,
Set up His home.
Now in my heart He finds room.

The way has been long,
Often so hard,
But He's been with me each day.

He has been faithful,
Lifting the gloom.
He's been there all the way.

Now I can sing,
Laugh and smile.
Jesus has taken control.

This is the same that
He wants for you,
A new life that's vital and whole.

Give Him your heart,
His grace He'll impart
Making you healthy and free.

He put my brokenness aright
He helps me walk in His pure light.
To comfort, bind, love and guide,
He'll always be there at my side.

He knows I've failed, for that He grieves,
Though He stands ready to intercede.
He's my most perfect Friend
Who'll stand beside me until the end.

No greater friend could there be
Than Jesus Who died on Calvary.
As I place my hand in His with trust
He removes the grime and dust.

He Who loves without a qualm
Will provide the healing balm.
Grace and pardon He gives anew;
As I trust in Jesus, He sees me through.

Gold

Tarnished from sin
Hollow within
I turned to my Lord.

"Lord, help me please!
I'm down on my knees,
Begging for You to come in."

He met me there,
Filled with my care,
Holding His hand out to me.

As to Him, I bow,
He teaches me how
To walk and live for Him.

Mistakes I still make
As my sins He does take,
Each day, giving comfort anew.

I love Him so,
As in Him I grow,
Loving Him more each day.

Replacing the old
My Lord, with His gold,
Covers each part anew.

Leaving behind
The tarnish of sin
He shines through my life.

It's not just a covering,
A plating of gold
Covering a hollow core.

My Lord does assure
It's solid clear through,
His plan is that and much more.

You'll shed the old
As He fills with His gold.
A new life you will find.

He will heal,
Renew, and redeem you,
Teaching you His will.

He'll give you treasure
For each bit of tarnish,
A shining for what was once dull.

His gold is not
Just a brittle facade,
It's solid gold clear through.

Out of the pit
Into new life.
He's waiting with love for you.

Rubble

As I sat among the rubble of the distant past,
Those years behind me . . . broken, filled with bitter tears,
My heart cried out to God's own Son
To help me with the life in Him
I'd only just begun.

Those years past
Still stormy,
Have caused a growth, a quietness to come.
The pain which seemed at one time so hard to bear
Is changing me, through His loving care.

Assurance floods my heart and soul!
His words are real. Through pain He heals,
Through sorrow and hurt come paths to a more mature life.
He's using such to make me whole.

I've often cried such bitter tears,
Sorrowing over the wasted years,
Clinging to my tattered life,
Filled with sorrow and so much strife.

Time's gone by since He came...
He has delicately severed and healed.
He's giving life meaning,
Showing what's real.

Through life's hurts
I've found my way to Him.
I will live eternally
For He has chosen me.

The Reality of Christ

God's forgiveness through Jesus Christ, His personal love and acceptance, His interest in the details and His plans for our lives are all a part of the reality of the Lord. He is always there . . . never too busy, never in a bad mood, always listening, always ready to forgive. He knew us before we were even born. Not one of us was an unwanted child. Regardless of our earthly background, we were planned and wanted by God.

Life is not always fair. Our illusions and expectations are frequently destroyed by the reality of life. However, we can still praise God because through each experience He can mold us and mature us, helping us to become more like Him. Every time we turn that bad experience over to Him, each crisis, failure or painful event, He can redeem and restore. Although this has been said often and may sound trite, as He begins to work in our lives, we start to see that these promises of God are filled with power. They are His LIVING WORD!

It is exciting to know that Jesus Christ is bigger than our problems, failures, or complexes, whether past, present or future. He is bigger than our finances, relatives, neighbors, problems with our children, fears, doubts, insecurities, crises, grief, our stained pasts and all the gigantic and minuscule problems in our lives. There is nothing too big and nothing too small for Him.

When I listen to nonbelievers moan about the status of the world, I can understand the frustration and hopelessness. Without Jesus Christ at the center of our existence, there is no meaning to life, no direction, no forgiveness, no prayer and no hope.

It is thrilling to know that in the crises and testing of my faith, God has been totally faithful. When that faith is challenged, He gives grace to help us come out strong.

Many times, understanding of the things God has done comes later. Looking back, it is often possible to see how He used the very things we thought were so bad to strengthen, mature and form us into His image. Sometimes, here on earth, we won't understand, but His Word remains true. He loves, cares for, reproves, guides, leads and forgives us.

The intellect cannot understand, but His Spirit reveals to us all we need to know. He does it in His way and in His timing, asking only that we trust Him.

As you read Psalm 139:1-18, think about it and allow the Holy Spirit to reveal His love and hope for you.

The Cry of the Heart

In a world where hope is drowned out by the stress of modern living and where the words of God have become "passé'," the cry of the heart for love, understanding and warmth is all the more poignant.

Silent deaths of hopes, dreams and sometimes even lives may occur only a few doors away. No one realized. Lives become distant and impersonal. "My schedule" becomes all-important. Appointments and busy lives may have become the substitute for friends and family. The cry is for love and hope.

Fear of even a few moments of lonely silence becomes a way of life. These are drowning people. These are people who are trying to shut out the cries of their lonely lives with overwork, overplay, over accumulation of material things, and busyness. Fear lurks everywhere.

Jesus Christ, Lord and Savior, offers not only hope but healing, wholeness and richness in every area of our lives that matters. He offers this not to a chosen few, but to all. He is the great Redeemer, redeeming not only our eternal lives, but also those things that bring so much agony. He redeems us from every pit, and uses all that happened for His glory and our good if we allow Him. Jesus Christ is not an instant cure to all our ills. He is the answer to everything about our lives.

It will demand honesty, hard work on our parts, and commitment to His way. The rewards are a brand new life, a new beginning, hope, healing of ourselves and our relationships (our part, at least), and the redemption of every part of our past that seems unredeemable. He gives fulfillment and a reason to live. He makes us rich in eternal things. He fills the void and heals the scars left by sin. His is a total love, acceptance and commitment. He is the answer to all we are craving and the One for Whom we are searching in our different ways.

No one is too young or too old, too sinful or too pure. Nothing matters to Him but your redemption. God loves you and me. He does not care how rich or poor we are. He looks deep into our hearts and sees our needs and insecurities. He whispers to us in those private places of fear and terror. He longs to take us, heal every area and set us free so that we might live anew for him. He waits for you and me. He is hope. He is love. He is life.

The Shoot

Bud of life,
Reaching a tiny finger to the sun,
Breaking through the soil, thirsting,
And hungering for the light.
In the journey upward, external forces reach
within the cool, dark prison of the soil.
Moisture to slake the thirst;
Sunlight to warm the earth,
Ever working on the tiny seed.

With time, a bit breaks through.
The confines of the seed are split,
And, life begins its way upward.
For a long period, this unseen growth is happening.
Then, suddenly, with strength and vigor,
The new sprout breaks through the soil,
Standing bent and bowed by the strain.

Day by day, as gentle waters soothe and refresh,
As the earth is warmed by the sun,
The tiny shoot reaches toward its Maker.
Hands lifted high in praise.
Shaking from itself the confines of the earth,
It grows daily closer to its Lord.

So let me be, dear Father,
As a tiny shoot,
Shaking off the grime of the world,
Daily refreshing through Your Word,
Taking it in to become a vital and living part of me.
Let me bring beauty and life to those around,
While growing ever closer to You.

The Chapel

Against the blue sky and billowy white clouds stands a sunshine-kissed chapel. It is really white but appears yellow in the sunlight. All around is green grass, multitudes of wild flowers and a lazy, winding road, curving upward toward the little house of God. Scattered here and there are lichen-spotted tombstones . . . ancient and covered with moss.

It exudes peace. The setting is quiet except for the subdued humming of the bees. There is a lack of pretense and a sense of the presence of God.

The upward climbing road has great chuckholes in places and a lot of dust. Sometimes the sun beats down mercilessly on that path, yet other portions of it are cool and refreshing. There are flat places where streams run across the trail. In some places, trees give shelter from the blazing sun. At the end of that narrow way, there is peace, joy and rest for the soul as well as the body.

Inside the chapel, it is cool and refreshing. The stillness is broken only by the sweet whisper of the Lord as He speaks peace to the heart.

The road leading to this peaceful chapel reminds of passages in God's Word speaking of the narrow road to heaven. That narrow way is often plagued with difficulties. There are dry times, when one is weary and parched. It also affords the refreshing coolness of God's promises, healed bodies and minds, spiritual growth and victory. It always leads upward, though we stumble and fall, to that sun-kissed chapel which represents the Lord Jesus Christ, the Author of peace.

The Strawberry

Ruby-red peaks out from
Moss-green leaves.
A jewel, growing in the middle
Of the spreading foliage.

Starting as a tiny plant,
Sun, rain, wind, cold and warmth,
Alternately assault and caress,
Bringing forth rapid growth of leaves.

These are followed by little buds
Which open to expose white petals.
The flowers drop off, leaving a hard, yellowish bud.
It increases in size until it is almost as large as my thumb.

First comes pale-green, then off-white and the first sign of pink.
Each day it ripens until the blood-red sheen
can be seen among the leaves.

Ripening fruit.
Lord, the ripening of the fruit of Your Spirit
Goes through a similar process.

We start out so small and immature,
But under Your guidance,
As we experience sunny days and storms in our lives,
Your fruit grows.

It never just appears ripe and luscious.
Ripened, mature fruit always comes through a growing process,
With ups and downs,
Calms and storms,
Heat and cold.

Luscious fruit finally appears
Jewel-like, fully developed, mature and
Tasty, to give glory to our God.

The Exchange

The mantle of judgment and criticism
Lay heavy upon my shoulders.
Intolerance and bigotry
Have many names.

Deep within me,
I knew this wasn't right.
At slightest provocation
I prepared to fight.

Gently Jesus spoke to me,
Let me know His love...
Then simply told me it must go,
This hatred in my heart.

He showed me how its roots had come,
But, now it is so wrong.
He doesn't want a burdened heart
To cloud work He wants done.

As I say "Yes" to His commands,
The Exchange begins.
The bitterness will turn to sweet,
The hatred, then to love.

The hurt and pain to healing,
To love for ones I've shunned.
To my blind eyes He gives sight,
And shackles are undone.

The little bit
That He requires
Is honesty with Him
And He forgives my sin.

Tiny Bird

Tiny bird,
Quiet and full of confidence
Sits in her nest,
Oblivious to the violent storm.

Limbs of trees toss,
Fling, and shake
Her world of
Sticks and grass.

Little bird,
Confident
That in the storm
Her God is near.

Dear Lord, please let me be
Like this tiny bird,
When all around me is
Shaking and churning.

Let me know You are near.
Let me rest
In utter trust,
Confident in Your care.

Covered by His Hand

Covered by the shadow of His hand
I walk in peace,
I walk in safety.

He has given me His words to speak,
Flowing through me
To you.

Words of life and healing,
Words of comfort too,
Words He means to bring peace and love.

Words of encouragement,
Words to teach us all,
Words to remind and to soothe.

Under the shadow of His hand,
I find that peace,
I find that safety.

Knowing that He protects from harm,
I take the hurt
That life hands out.

Thank You my Father,
Thank You my Lord.
Thank You for giving me Your Word.

Safe beneath the shadow of Your hand,
I learn to live,
I learn to give.

Inspired by Isaiah 51:16.

Deep Pools

Deep pools of water
Reflect the soul within.
Sometimes stormy, sometimes calm,
Sometimes filled with sin.

Quiet times of reflection,
Raging times of emotion,
Deep pools of water
Mirror the soul within.

Water muddied as I perceive
Myself through troubled eyes.
Crystal clear and sparkling
When seen through Jesus Christ.

Jesus, Lord and Savior
Please cleanse these pools of mine.
Replace the soiled water.
Let purity clearly shine.

Deep pools of water
Reflect the soul within.
Given to my Savior,
To remove the stains of sin.

Lord, let my pools of water
Be cleansed and pure to see.
Let Your love flow through them
For all eternity.

As Close as Your Breath

"As close as your breath,"
He whispered to me,
"Is where I am each day."

"My love is so near,
Residing within,
It never goes away."

"No matter your feelings,
No matter your mood,
I'm close as I can be."

"Trust in My Word,
Not how you feel,
At times when you do not see."

"I'm close as your breath.
I live within.
I'll never go away."

Friends

It seems as though they are all around.
Everybody seems to have friends, or do they?
Friends is a word often taken lightly,
But, when you don't have one, there is poverty in your soul.
A deep force which either drives you to reach out to another,
Or, forces you deep inside yourself where no one can reach,
And pain cannot touch you.

Life is different with a friend,
More complete somehow.
To know that someone else cares when all else is in ruins
May make the difference in your will to go on.

To be a friend is an even more rare experience,
One not to be taken lightly or tampered with.
To be a friend can be so richly rewarding.
Reaching out and touching a heart that aches and longs for love,
One which grows more unattractive each time it is shunned,
That is being a friend.

A special warmth comes in loving another, no matter how seemingly
insignificant.
That smile you gave today may have been a ray of hope to one who was
very low.
That time you stopped to listen or placed your hand on that unwashed
sleeve.
At the time when God's compassion flowed through you, reaching
through the agony and the tears began to flow; that is to be a friend; that
is to love a neighbor.

The time you laughed, rejoiced and shared the joy as you entered into
another's world,
You were a friend.

You listened, no matter that the story was dull. It wasn't important that
you had heard it so often.
No matter the hour, you were always there to hear what had to be said or
left unsaid.

You stood by that person's side when grief overwhelmed and not a word could be uttered. You held that wrinkled hand as death closed in. That was being a friend.

Lord, this I ask, let me have the joy of **having** a friend, but more important; let me have the privilege of **being** a friend.

Chapter 9:

GOD'S CREATION

Blindness
Wondrous Creation
Encounter
His Creation
Heavenly Gifts
Pageant
Cloak of Many Colors
Glistening Explosion
Beauty/Ugliness
Bits of Beauty
There is Beauty
The Gossamer Veil
Clouds
Cascade
Life Is Like the Weather
Weather and Me
Fog
Summer Rain
Wind
New Beginnings

Blindness

Strip away the blindness
of my heart's eyes,
Father, and let me partake of
Your glorious creation!

Wondrous Creation

A sighing breeze
Through a grove of trees . . .

A tiny bird
Flitting from branch to branch . . .

The rippling sound
Of water in a brook . . .

Daylight
Following hours of dark . . .

Bright, spring flowers
Following the dreariness of winter . . .

Lord, Your creation
Is so wondrous!

Words cannot express
The love I feel for You.

Encounter

There was a crystal moment for me today. It was a time of oneness with the earth, with my soul and with my Creator. I was lying in the grass, gazing up through the tree's limbs and leaves. All above me was the loveliest blue with great fluffy clouds scattered here and there. The sun baked my face. As I looked straight ahead, all that was visible was a mass of waving grain. All that was audible was the hum of insects and an occasional song from a bird. There was also the wind, so soft and cool and nothing more than a caress at that level. It was just enough to refresh me.

The golden sun was suddenly covered by a massive black cloud. Seeming very helpless, the sun appeared to be swallowed by the cloud. Becoming oblivious to all else, my whole concentration centered on that scene. It was a beautiful moment. The cloud swirled, snaked back on itself, danced, and then whirled angrily about, devouring the sun. It was as though I were gazing into the midst of a giant, seething, swirling cauldron!

At that height, the wind was more than a mere whisper. It sent the clouds up, down and around in a frenzied dance. I felt I was present at creation . . . an awesome moment . . . even greater because I was so close to home. All that beauty and majesty was there, just waiting for me to take time out of my routine tasks to see and experience it.

Then, from the depths of blackness came a wan light. Steadily it came, growing brighter and more golden. Suddenly, the sun burst from its prison! Shining once again, it gave heat, life and glory.

There was a message for me there too. As I emerge from the blackness, from the depths of the prison of depression, I am becoming brighter. I, too, shall burst forth in joy and life, able to bring warmth and life to those around me. I treasure those moments stolen from a busy routine. I was taken backward in time to a simpler day. As a child, I would lie beneath an apple tree, hear the hum of insects, feel the warmth of the sun upon my face and I was comforted.

His Creation

So many times, in my personal and spiritual life, I witness the brilliance of Jesus flashing through the grayness. He grows greater and brighter, lighting up my entire life. I seem to radiate Him.

Then experiences come that seem to extinguish every trace of warmth, color and glow. Dimness settles upon me. Heavy clouds surround my life.

Through all of it comes Jesus, my own great, fiery Orb, to lift the clouds, bring warmth and spiritual light, just as the sun does to the earth.

How often I have found the correlation between Nature and spiritual life. God, the Author of both, can teach me so much through His creation.

Pageant

Fascinated, I sat at my window,
As God performed the pageant of sunrise.
Breathtakingly beautiful hues,
A rainbow of color,
Exploding upward until the sky was filled
With the joyous cry of another day!

Cloak of Many Colors

The sky flings out its cloak of many colors
And cries....IT IS DAY!

Glistening Explosion

Dark tree limbs, weeping droplets of water,
Explode with glistening light
As the sun shines upon them.

Blinding in their beauty,
A thousand shimmering diamonds
Sparkle in the sudden light.
Thank You, Lord for the riches of beauty
In the everyday things of life.

Beauty/Ugliness

Destinies of hundreds of thousands are being lived out under the twinkling lights of the city. People from every walk of life live there. There are the decent, the kind, the predators, the sick, the well, old people, babies, children, life and death.

The lines of cars on the darkened freeway appear as beautiful chains of rubies on one side . . . strands of glistening white pearls on the other. Inside are tired, impatient people who see no beauty in a traffic jam.

Ugly gray skies and blustery November winds contrast with a brilliantly colored red-gold leaf lying on the sidewalk. Its beauty lifts a burdened heart.

So often, beauty and ugliness go hand in hand. One is there close to the other. Oh, Lord, help me to see the beauty in life, especially in those times when it seems so ugly.

Bits of Beauty

Bits of red, dotted with black
Glisten against vibrant green leaves.

God's tiny creatures,
The ladybugs,
Bless my heart.

There Is Beauty

There is beauty in this world.
It's everywhere, just look around you.

See the colored shells in shades of coral, yellow, blue and pink. Stripes and tiny tracings of brown and black paint a canvas of pale yellow.

See the rose, tightly closed, then waking to the morning sun, yawning and opening to show its beauty to each passerby.

Breathe in the scents of freshly clipped grass, the aroma of newly baked bread and freshly brewed coffee at that hour of awakening.

Observe the moon, full or only part, especially when framed by giant thunderclouds.

Revel in the sun, particularly precious following weeks of gray and gloom. Suddenly the world looks brighter, the grass greener and the sky bluer.

See the tiny ladybug, beloved by all, climbing laboriously over the fresh green leaves.

Hear the sound of children laughing, enjoying life with a zest we despair of, yet envy.

Life is beautiful and life is ugly. It depends upon which side of the leaf we choose to look . . . on what things we allow our minds to dwell.
Life is peace and life is anguish. So often, the anguish is in our minds and many of the fears are mere imaginings. Many times, peace is pushed aside so that we can dwell on those things in the past, present or future, over which we have no control. These are so often things we fear which never come to pass.

Feel the breeze whipping your hair about your face. Cry out to God, "I want to live for You! I want to feel! I am alive!" You see, life can be beautiful.

The Gossamer Veil

At the sound of the alarm, I tumbled out of bed. Tripping and stumbling down the hallway, I opened the curtains. Before me was dazzling beauty.

A gossamer veil of mist hovered over the lake. Moonlight illuminated the mist. The brilliant light filtered through the vapor, making thousands of sparkling diamonds reflect from the black lake. As though a floodlight shone, it radiated throughout the low-lying fog.

I too, can be like the mist. As Jesus shines His light on me, I can spread it to each around me, allowing Him to bring forth sparkling diamonds in this dark world.

Clouds

Glorious clouds.
Billowy masses piled high in the sky,
Reflect the splendor of the rising sun.

Brilliant gold, red and pink
Streak the mass,
Illuminating the still dark sky.

As the sun rises,
The light is diffused.
The clouds turn to pastels,
Reaching colorful fingers across the sky,
Welcoming the budding day.

Glorious clouds,
Clouds of splendor,
Heralding the return of our Lord Jesus Christ.
Each morning a reminder of His promise to come again...
Extending fingers of hope and joy
Into each newborn day.

RHEINFALL, SWITZERLAND

Cascade

Streams of refreshing water
Cascading in my soul.
Streams of healing water
Making my life whole.

My Lord sent this water
Causing flowers to bloom,
Where there was only wasteland,
Bitterness and gloom.

All around are hurting people,
Not knowing that they thirst,
Reaching out their futile cups,
Trying to be first.

Lord, let Your living streams
Flow through me to them.
Heal and touch their hopeless hearts,
Help them live again.

Life Is Like the Weather

Life is like the weather. Very few spring days occur with birds singing, balmy temperature, pretty flowers, sunny skies, and no clouds.

Occasionally we have days like that and really appreciate them. However, it is unrealistic to expect a life full of this sort of spring days.

Life is full of storms (big crises), fog (times of depression), ice and snow (death and mourning), brilliant colors (happy occasions) and soft, sunny days (contented, peaceful times).

All of them make up growth and life. Where it is always sunny, life dies. When there is too much rain, life also dies. We need all the phases of weather in our lives for healthy growth. Praise You, Lord for the miracle of weather and life.

Weather and Me

Minute droplets of water fall softly to the ground,
nuzzling the grass and twigs and twining themselves
around every available thing.

Fog, dew, frost, rain, water soothe the thirst,
Coat, nourish, cleanse and wash away the clutter.

The sky closes in and seems to wrap itself around each house.
The view is blurred; I find peace and quiet.

The weather often finds a counterpart in my life.
Moments of darkness. These times are inky black with no moon.
Other dark times are illumined by a bright moon and twinkling stars.

Cold. Sometimes it is a coldness of the soul going
straight to the marrow. Other times, it is a coldness brightened
by crystal clear air, sunny skies, and frosty breath. This cold,
brings pinkness to cheeks and new awareness of the beauty
of God's world.

Sun. These are times when I cannot shout
my joy enough. They are warm,
sunny, carefree, happy and giggly. Other sunny days cause sweating over
every small task. The heat seems endless and unbearable and I long for
thirst-quenching rains and cloudy days.

My being is also made up of seasons that change as often as the weather.
Even as You made the weather Lord, You made me. I am stormy,
sunny, light, dark, peaceful, blustery, mild . . . a mosaic of
wonderful emotions.

Fog

A cold, opaque mantle settled upon everything,
Muffling sounds and distorting vision. Sometimes it was
impossible to see anything.
Quiet, downy-soft, wrapping its gentle white fingers
about one as a scarf.
Deep quiet . . . an eerie, yet, soothing atmosphere.
The light in a house seems cheerier,
the fire warmer and
the sounds of humanity dearer.

Sometimes, a season of fog comes into one's life,
casting cold, quiet, impersonal feelings within.
One is left wandering about a bit befuddled,
drawing nearer to the familiar, to the warmth.
Feeling isolated, alone, fearful, a bit confused,
In blindness, one sometimes stumbles, falls
or runs into things.

Then comes the sun and a little breeze,
clearing away the fog.
All seems more dear and there is appreciation for the
warmth and clear skies.
Fogs are necessary, but never forever.
The fogs come and the fogs go,
and always comes the sun.

Dark moments, moments of torment and confusion
come; that's inevitable.
The sun always comes and eventually sweeps the fog away.
It leaves one stronger, wiser, more loving and
understanding of others whose lives are now in fog.

At this time, we, the veterans of other foggy times
can bring some warmth into their lonely lives.

Summer Rain

Soft showers are falling . . . tender showers from heaven.
They are cleansing showers, soothing showers,
precious . . . from God Himself.

Have you ever noticed how everything looks so green and lush
following a summer rain? Dust is gone and thirst is quenched.
All is refreshed. Then, out comes the sun, causing cobwebs to
appear as jewel-laden necklaces. Diamonds seem to sparkle on every
blade of grass.

Everything in nature seems to have a spiritual application. We can
learn more about God if we only look around.

God sends His rain into our lives too or allows it to happen at times.
We receive summer showers, heavy rainfall
and sometimes wild downpours.
They can either drown us or cause us to sparkle.

During the rain, we can turn our faces to our Creator and let Him
cleanse us. No doubt, the raindrops upon a fragile flower are painful.
Yet the flower flourishes and is beautified by even a painful experience.

Our rains pass too. If we have drawn close to Jesus,
we will be refreshed, made softer and lovelier. When He brings
forth His Son, we shall stand brilliant and sparkling in His light.

Wind

It is quiet and I am alone with God.
What a precious time, a golden moment on which to hang.
I am loath to go to bed, though my body is sagging with weariness.
I don't want this moment to end.

The wind wraps its fingers around the branches, and pushes
the surface of the lake in time with the clouds. As
though bent on some important mission, they race.

The wind blows so hard, it almost frightens me.
Trees assume grotesque yet awesome positions
as they whip this way and that.

The Holy Spirit, symbolically the wind, blows through my life.
He sweeps away cobwebs and churns up dirt that needs removal.
Frightful anxiety overcomes me at times as He severs broken limbs
and rotten branches in my life . . . the debris of sin. When
the storm passes, He blows lightly and coolly across my flushed
cheeks and fevered brow, and lulls me to
peaceful slumber, safe in His arms.

New Beginnings

Winter snows, storms, frosts and winds give way to spring. New
life erupts out of storm-lashed and buffeted trees and shrubs.
God's promises come to mind. He brings beauty out of
seeming ugliness and life out of seeming death.

You may be in a winter time in your life.
Circumstances may have brought
you low and sown seeds of doubt and confusion. You feel used,
dried out and faint. Take heart. Our precious Lord is stirring up new
life within you. He uses all the storms, heartaches, struggles and
tragedies to bring you to maturity in Christ. The fruits of the Spirit
can only grow because of the winters in your life. It is a necessary
time to perfect the bloom and eventually the fully mature fruit.

Praise God for spring! Praise His name for new beginnings, no matter
how stormy the past.

A new beginning is available to each, no
matter the failure or sins of the past.
As these parts of your life are turned over to Him to redeem and if
you make Him Lord and Savior of your life, you
can experience a new beginning in Christ.

Chapter 10:

Praise and Worship

Precious Lord
Sunday Morning
Rejoice
Little Rosebud
Falling Tears
Joy

Precious Lord

Precious Lord, my heart swells with love and gratitude for the
hope and promises to be found in You.

You love me. Down to the tiniest, most insignificant concern,
You are interested. You care. You are watching, guarding, loving,
Healing and nurturing.

In You I find protection, truth, love, acceptance and renewal.
For these things, I thank You Father.

Sunday Morning

Sun filters through
Majestic standing trees.
Uninhibited worship in song
As the Spirit takes hold.

Worship . . . rising to heaven
Above as believers
Pour out their love
To God.

Rejoice

Rejoice!
Rejoicing in You!
Lord, I rejoice in Your love.

Rejoice!
Rejoicing in You!
Father, I rejoice in You.

Living a life
That is sometimes so hard,
Learning new lessons each day,

I turn to You
With a question or doubt;
I turn to You with my joy.

Rejoice!
Rejoicing in You,
I rejoice in You.

Circumstances come,
Fear fills my heart,
You seem far away.

Then comes the light,
Piercing the gloom.
You're just one prayer away.

Rejoice!
Rejoicing in You!
I rejoice in You.

Rejoice!
Rejoicing in You!
I rejoice in You.

Rejoice!

Little Rosebud

I saw a little rosebud . . . a splash of crimson against vivid green.
It seemed so incongruous. This lovely bloom, glorious in beauty
and scent, comes from the most insignificant of rosebushes.

The weeds have nearly crowded out this bush's
life. The stems are so spindly
the full bloom bows the stalk to the ground.
It reminds me, Lord, of what You can do with our
seemingly insignificant lives. We seem so puny
and sickly on the outside, surrounded
by weeds of sin and the world's evil. Yet, out of these lives, You can
make a breath-taking blossom . . . one which brings joy to all around.

The rose is totally exposed to the weather.
It has been mowed by mistake, stepped on, buffeted by winter's frigid
winds and baked by summer's sun, yet You
have made its blossom perfection.

Your loving hands have taken this insignificant, homely,
pest-beset plant, formed crimson velvet petals and gave them
heavenly perfume.
When You do that for the rose, regardless of what the
bush looks like, we can be assured You will do the
same for our damaged lives, if we only ask.

Thank You, God for Your transforming power. You bring strength out of
weakness, beauty out of destruction and fragrance out of moldering lives.

Falling Tears

Tears fall as rain
As I consider the blessings
You pour out on me.

Lord, they are not tears of pain.
I am simply so touched
You want to use me.

For so many years,
The tears were for
The shattered life I'd led.

You are making me whole,
Using me
To touch other lives,

To give hope, healing
And freedom
As You work through my life.

Thank You, Lord.
The tears I bring are
Tears of thanksgiving and joy.

Joy

Joy bursts forth
In the song of a bird
Trilling out his pleasure
With his world.

Joy bursts forth
From my pen with this word,
Sharing the overflowing
Of my heart.

God touched me
In an area of pain.
He showed me how He
Longs to set me free.

I'm being robbed,
But, not only me.
Christ, my world and
My family is too.

Being loosed from a burden
I've carried all my life,
Loosed by the power of
His Word.

Loosed from this burden
Through the love
Of His children who
Faithfully pray for me.

Thank You my Lord,
My God, My King.
Let my joy
Through these praises ring!

Rich am I...
Beyond compare.
Thank You, dear Lord,

For Your tender care.
Joy and rapture
fill my heart.
Deeper joy
When rapture departs.

He is still there
Covering me,
With healing in His wings,
He's setting me free.

Accepting Jesus Christ As Your Personal Savior

If you have not yet accepted Jesus Christ as your personal Lord and Savior, you can do that now by just uttering a simple prayer. As you pray for Him to come into your life as personal Savior, ask Him to forgive your sins and become Lord of your life, you become His child. Please be sure to get in touch with a Bible -believing church where you can learn more about His Word and what He wants for your life.

Date I accepted Jesus as my personal Savior:

_____

Epilogue

God has taken each ugly and hurtful thing I have brought Him and He has redeemed it. His faithfulness through those times of pain, sorrow and hurt, His steady nearness and His great love have all worked miracles in my heart. The problems don't always go away. I continue to struggle mightily at times, but He is always with me.

What He has done before, He will do again. He will see each person who desires it through the dry times and the hard times. My prayer is that we all realize we are not alone in painful times. If we know Him as personal Savior and Lord, He can use every experience, no matter how horrible, to heal us, give us more compassion for others, bring maturity and help us comfort the hurting.

Ours is a great God!

I shout my praise!

HALLELUJAH!
Crystal J. Ortmann

CPSIA information can be obtained at www.ICGtesting.com
Printed in the USA
BVOW022327131212

308141BV00003B/273/P